The OCD Breakthrough Workbook for Teenagers: Triumph Over Intrusive Thoughts and Compulsive Behaviors

Free your mind, Empower Your True Self, and Unleash Your Full Potential

Cross Border Books

Table of Contents

Introduction

OCD is a phrase that is thrown around a lot... People on social media of all ages claim to have the condition and use it as an excuse for poor behaviors or even as a reason for the bad habits they have formed.

For those who have OCD, these loose phrases and broad statements are an insult—we want to scream, "OCD is real, it's a mental health condition, and it dramatically affects our lives!"

But we don't because those who are lucky enough not to have the disorder aren't aware of how our obsessions, anxieties, compulsions, and rituals rob us of thriving in our own lives. Or how having manageable symptoms that don't directly affect our day-to-day routines can still cause us distress and extreme anxiety.

A lot of the time, having OCD can make us feel like we are puppets and our actions are governed by the puppet master that is our brain. It's a stressful cycle of thoughts dominating actions and rituals that dominate every facet of our lives. If you're here and you're reading this workbook after reading *Calm the Chaos! Overcoming OCD for Teenagers*: I applaud you for taking the next step in regaining your life.

And, if you're new to this series or haven't yet read the previous book, welcome... I am positive you will learn a lot about your condition and a whole lot of tools to help take back your life.

Before you begin with the exercises in this book, I'd like you to know that you're not alone. One in every five hundred kids in the United States alone has been diagnosed with OCD, and a whole lot more haven't yet sought out treatment (Zauderer, 2023). This brings me to my next point.

If you think you have OCD, speak with an adult in your life so that they can get you to a mental health provider who will properly assess you. OCD is characterized by thoughts that cause anxiety. These can be thoughts that cause fear about how things are, how they could end up, or even how things *should* be.

Now, this doesn't seem too bad, but with OCD, these thoughts are persistent and run through your mind over and over again. This is called rumination, and often ruminating thoughts don't make any sense and are simply not true.

To rid ourselves of these thoughts, we begin to develop compulsive behaviors aimed at preventing them from reoccupying our minds over and over again. Often, these behaviors will be things we do to try and create a safe space for ourselves or prevent something bad from happening.

For example, if you're having obsessive thoughts about germs, you may wash your hands in a set pattern or ritual to prevent germs from being on your hands. I will guide you through these obsessions and compulsions throughout the course of this book, so you don't have to get too caught up in the details yet. For now, it's important for you to know that some rumination is normal, too much rumination is not great, and compulsions as a result of rumination are OCD.

Right, so now that you have an idea of what OCD is, let's look at what *Free your mind, Empower Your True Self, and Unleash Your Full Potential* are about and how it can help you reclaim your life.

Creating my OCD books was a journey for me, one in which I was able to explore my own OCD while revisiting some of the tools and techniques that really worked for me in managing my OCD symptoms.

During this writing journey, I made the decision to help others reach their goals of breaking free from OCD so that they too, could achieve success, but I didn't want to drown my readers in too much information.

Book 1, *Calm the Chaos! Overcoming OCD for Teenagers* focused on the ins and outs of OCD and the science behind the condition. It also contained some worksheets with exercises that could be used to manage the symptoms of OCD.

But I didn't want to only teach teens how to manage their symptoms; I wanted them to become an unstoppable force in defeating their OCD! So I got to formulating some of the most effective therapeutic exercises that have been proven to help teens conquer their obsessive thoughts. And this is what you're reading now.

Each of the exercises contained in this book has been thoughtfully chosen and curated for you... no adult stuff here... so that you can begin your journey to mental wellness and a life free of overwhelming thoughts and time-consuming rituals.

Finally, before you dive into the chapters below, I'd like you to know that you're not defined by your disease. You are not OCD—you have OCD, and you're certainly not odd or weird, and you definitely didn't do anything wrong.

None of this is your fault, nor does your OCD need to continue to limit your amazing presence on this spinning globe we call Earth. You have the potential to do incredible things with your life, and with a little guidance, some help, and the exercises contained within this book, OCD doesn't need to be yet another obstacle you need to overcome. So, if you're ready, grab a pen and a notebook, unleash your potential, embrace your authentic self, and let's step out of the darkness into the light together.

Chapter 1:
Cognitive Behavioral Therapy for OCD

Cognitive behavioral therapy (CBT) is a form of talk therapy that is used to help manage the behaviors that result from our thoughts. It's important that you know that CBT doesn't cure conditions.

Rather, it is used to manage the symptoms of mental and some physical health disorders by changing thought patterns. Before I get into how CBT works, I would like to introduce you to a concept that may be new to you.

I'd like you to take a moment to think back to a time when you did something that you knew you shouldn't have done. This could be not studying for a test, playing games when your parents asked you not to, and so on.

What you did back then is obviously irrelevant now, but if you think back to that time, chances are you'll remember that not only were your thoughts racing, but your body probably felt weird too. Perhaps you had a strange feeling in your belly; your heart was racing; you may have developed a headache; your palms may have started to sweat, and you could have even felt nauseous.

And all of these physical and emotional responses have happened as a response to your behavior and your thoughts about your behavior. Chances are, if you fessed up to what you had done, all of those weird feelings in your body would disappear as soon as the consequences of your actions became clear.

This is called "psychosomatic-related illness," and it has been studied a lot by the mental and physical health industry because the effects your thoughts have on your brain, behaviors, and body need to be better understood (Zauderer, 2023).

Once you have a better understanding of how profoundly your thoughts can affect your body, it becomes a little bit easier to understand why managing your thoughts and changing your perspectives can directly affect your behaviors. And this is what CBT is all about. It's the connection between how we think, feel, and behave and the negative thoughts that affect our everyday lives. The goal of doing CBT exercises and practicing them often is to help us deal with the overwhelming thoughts we can sometimes have in a more constructive, positive way. Sometimes this is done by breaking these thoughts down into smaller parts, and other times it is done by confronting these thoughts with facts. All of this might sound like a hard task, especially when we're stuck in negative thought patterns like obsessions, but CBT is a very, very effective tool you can use to help reframe your thoughts and break the destructive path of obsessive thoughts.

So how is CBT different from other talk therapies?

CBT specifically focuses on the present and doesn't seek to uncover past factors that may have contributed to our thoughts, compulsions, and behaviors. Because of this, CBT is incredibly effective in treating a lot of disorders, including OCD. CBT is such an effective treatment that it is even used by people who have chronic health issues like irritable bowel syndrome and fibromyalgia to help manage stress, anxiety, and chronic pain.

Doing CBT exercises may not be a cure for OCD, but it is the gold standard in the treatment and management of its symptoms. By confronting thought patterns head-on and halting the obsessive spirals that dominate OCD, anyone is able to better manage their behaviors and compulsions.

CBT Exercises to Help You Manage Your OCD

Now you know that CBT is very effective in changing our thought patterns and challenging our thought spirals. Questioning our thoughts with curiosity and compassion is vitally important for our mental health and is the first step in being able to manage our behaviors and compulsions.

You will notice that I have not used the words "control" or "cure" when speaking about CBT when speaking about OCD and the exercises you will do to empower yourself. The reason for this is that OCD is a lifelong condition that cannot be cured, but it can be managed, and you don't need to be a slave to your compulsions or the thoughts you're having forever.

My suggestion for completing these exercises is to choose a time when you're going to be uninterrupted and can really reflect upon your thoughts as well as your way forward. Added to this, I'd like you to grab your journal right now and think about your reason for wanting to become a master at managing your OCD.

This could be something as simple as wanting to live a better quality of life, getting into a university of your choice, or even trying to improve your personal relationships. Having a goal is really important for anything we do in life, as it provides us with the reasons *why* we're doing what we're doing. Now that you've written down your goals and are ready let's begin with CBT exercises that will help you manage your compulsions and thoughts.

CBT Exercises to Manage Your Obsessions

The exercises below are designed for you to complete in your own time. It's a good idea to keep all of these completed exercises, as well as a blank template so that you have access to the exercise at a moment's notice.

If you're more of a physical person, feel free to create your own tables in your journal so that you can complete each of them. Remember, there is no right or wrong way to think, and your goal when doing these exercises is *not* to judge yourself but to give yourself grace and love yourself through this process.

If you find your inner critic or that little negative voice in your head becoming nasty to you, ask it to kindly take a seat in the corner or let it know that your exercise time is a judgment-free zone!

CBT Exercise 1: Observing Your Thoughts— Functional Analysis

The ABC Functional Analysis worksheet is an exercise designed to help you explore your thoughts by examining cause and effect. For you to complete this exercise, you will need to collect the information your brain is feeding you so that you can uncover the *why* behind your compulsions.

Each column is labeled with a prompt. These columns are thought, antecedents (what caused the thought), behavior, and consequence, and below the prompt is an example of a possible answer.

Try not to rush through the process of identifying the antecedent and the consequence. If you already know the thought and the behavior, fill these in first and then sit in silence so that you can think about the cause and the consequence.

Thought	Antecedent	Behavior	Consequence
I need to get an A on this test	I had difficulty grasping a concept	I went over the concept all night	I am exhausted and can't concentrate

CBT Exercise 2: Dysfunctional Thought Record

This exercise will help you gain insight into your negative thoughts and figure out when they're most likely to cause you to struggle. A lot of the time, OCD thoughts are triggered by our environment or our behaviors.

In uncovering what situations are causing automotive thoughts, it becomes far easier for us to address them and put them to bed in a constructive way rather than letting them manifest as compulsions.

Because our compulsions are driven by our dysfunctional thoughts, creating a record of how we think can be highly beneficial to identifying our triggers. Added to this, by learning to challenge these thoughts and uncover what cognitive distortions are associated with our behaviors, we can begin to take the right steps toward freeing ourselves from our compulsions.

Often, the best way to uncover how our thoughts are affecting our behaviors is to uncover the facts and ascertain what the outcomes of these thoughts are rather than imagining all of the endless scenarios that play over and over in our heads.

As with the worksheet above, fill in each column, beginning with the date and time of your thought. Because our thoughts can sometimes compound or build, it can be difficult to keep track of what initial thought triggered the pattern we are in. As such, it may be a good idea to keep a copy of this exercise with you so that you can write down the date, time, and how you feel immediately.

The remainder of the columns can be filled in later if you do not have the time in the moment to analyze what cognitive distortion (thought lie) is present or the specific dysfunctional thought.

Date and Time	Where or what caused the thought?	What is the thought?	What emotions am I feeling?	What is the cognitive distortion?	What are the facts about this thought?	What was the outcome of my thoughts?

CBT Exercise 3: Fact-Checking Thoughts

Teens with OCD tend to have a common set of cognitive distortions or incorrect thoughts that trigger compulsions. Oftentimes, we tend to think that these thoughts directly relate to the thing we can identify.

An example of this would be washing our hands compulsively. We may think that we will get sick because we have touched something and, misleadingly, believe that the thought that triggered our compulsion is that our hands are dirty. When we become introspective and begin to question why we believe our hands are dirty, we uncover other stressors or thoughts that are directly responsible for our behaviors. And these thoughts are our cognitive distortions that need to be uncovered. In essence, they're the beliefs we have that drive both our thoughts and our behaviors.

Now, before you feel despondent about uncovering your beliefs, it's important that you understand that beliefs are not facts. They're simply a summary of our life experiences that have us thinking in a certain way.

A lot of us have had beliefs throughout the course of our lives that have changed over time as we have accumulated more knowledge. The entire nature of a belief is that it can change, and that's great news for you and your negative beliefs.

When filling out the table below, I want you to be as honest as possible. If you really believe that you're not intelligent, then mark the yes column. Don't rely on what others have told you; rely only on your beliefs.

Statement	Yes	No
I'm dumb/stupid/not intelligent		
I'm not pretty/handsome/attractive		
Nobody actually likes/loves me		
I have no friends		
I'm selfish		
This isn't going to work		
I am going to fail		
I am too fat/thin		
I am not good enough		
I will be alone forever		
I dislike my life		
People are disappointed in me		
I am not good at anything/have no strengths		
There is no point in anything		

The things you ticked off in the yes column are cognitive distortions and will require you to restructure your thought patterns using Exercise 4.

CBT Exercise 4: Cognitive Restructuring—Changing How You Think

Cognitive restructuring is the ability to change our untrue thoughts by challenging them with facts. Because our thoughts are deeply rooted in what we believe, the only way to change them is to ascertain whether they're true or not. And, even if they are true, once you know what the thought is, you've uncovered a subconscious concern you have.

Let's say you have ticked off "you don't like your life." You will now know there is something about the way you are living that isn't quite sitting right with your mind, and you have the choice to choose it. Now that you know how cognitive restructuring works, grab a pen, pencil, or your typing fingers and complete the exercise below.

What is my thought?	What are the facts supporting my thought?	What are the facts contradicting my thought?

Now, answer the questions below

1. Is my thought based on evidence, or is this my opinion?

2. Is the situation as black-and-white as it seems?

3. Could I be wrong about the facts?

4. Could others have a different perspective?

5. Have I considered all of the facts and not just supporting facts?

6. Am I over-inflating the facts?

7. Am I entertaining my thoughts even though I know they're false?

8. How reliable is the source of these facts? Is it someone's opinion or my own opinion?

9. How likely is it that these thoughts are true?

Answering these questions will help you uncover the truth about your thoughts and assist you in either dispelling them completely or making changes that improve your quality of life.

CBT Exercise 5: Mindful Meditation

One of the most popular techniques used in CBT to help interrupt a thought spiral, calm anxiety, and stop panic attacks in their tracks is mindful meditation. One form of mindful meditation is grounded meditation, which helps us remain in the present moment.

The easiest of these techniques for teens to learn is the 5-4-3-2-1 method. It can be done any time, any place, and it is really effective in distracting our minds long enough for a thought spiral to be broken.

Here's how to do it:

1. Take a deep breath through your nose and exhale through your mouth.
2. Open your eyes and focus on your breath.
3. Begin by looking around your surroundings and finding 5 things you see.
4. Say these 5 things out loud.
5. Move your attention to 4 things you can feel.
6. Touch each of these things and say them out loud.
7. Draw your attention to 3 things you can hear.
8. Listen to these things for a count of five and say them out loud.
9. Now, name 2 things you can smell.
10. Notice the aroma of these 2 things and say them out loud.
11. Finally, name 1 thing you can taste.
12. Say it out loud.

If your mind hasn't calmed sufficiently by the time, you have gone down the list, repeat steps 1 through 12, choosing different objects in your environment this time.

CBT Exercises to Help You Manage Your Compulsions

Our compulsive behaviors are grounded in anxiety and panic as a response to our thoughts. They're the things we do to try and soothe our mind and our body as we go through a fear response that feels like it's never-ending.

CBT uses redirection and your body's own natural coping mechanisms to not only calm your mind but also manage your compulsions by temporarily offering a distraction and incorporating relaxation techniques.

While CBT is effective in helping to uncover our cognitive distortions, its true power comes from its ability to teach us to gain control over our bodies' reactions to our emotions, thoughts, and environment. The exercises below need to be practiced, however, and you're going to need to put effort into dealing with your thoughts first.

Having said that, these exercises will help you to calm yourself during your fear responses so that you feel more in control of the situation and can focus on correcting your cognitive distortions.

CBT Exercise 6: Progressive Muscle Relaxation (PMR)

This form of grounding exercise is a great way to become physically aware of your body and the type of fear response you may be having. It's important that we learn to interrupt our compulsions before we begin with the behaviors, and PMR is an excellent tool for helping you relax and convince your body and mind to break the fight-or-flight response you're in. In a way, you're training your body to disengage from an unhealthy response it's currently experiencing.

Method

It's best to practice PMR in a quiet space where you will be uninterrupted, but if you're in the midst of a panic attack or want to break the pattern of a compulsive behavior in the moment, try to stand still so that you can begin the exercise:

1. Stand rooted on the spot, sit comfortably, or lie down on your bed.

2. Close your eyes and take a deep breath, exhaling when you're ready.

3. Now, inhale through your nose until you feel your lungs expand to full capacity, and exhale through your mouth. Don't worry if you cannot take deep breaths; to begin with, shallow breathing is a symptom of your fear response.

4. Repeat your breaths, inhaling through your nose and exhaling through your mouth. Do this five times.

5. On your sixth inhale, squeeze the muscles in your toes and feet… hold it for a count of four.

6. Exhale through your mouth and release your muscles.

7. And… inhale through your nose, squeeze your calf muscles… hold it for a count of four.

8. Exhale through your mouth and release your muscles.

9. Repeat this process for your thighs, buttocks, belly, and arms, all the way down to your hands and fingers.

10. To end your PMR exercise, inhale through your nose and clench your jaw, scrunching your facial muscles in the process.

11. Exhale through your mouth and release your muscles.

12. If you're standing, give your body a little shake, just like a dog drying itself after getting wet.

Stop inhaling and exhaling deeply, but do take a moment to focus on your breath. Notice how your body feels… Now, open your eyes and gently begin moving about again.

CBT Exercise 7: Diaphragmatic Breathing

Also called belly breathing, this CBT technique sends an extremely strong message to your brain to calm both the body and mind down. While belly breathing is best done in a quiet spot, it's not an absolute necessity. What is important is that you are sitting or lying down when you complete the exercise, as you may begin to feel dizzy.

Instructions

1. Sit or lie down.

2. Place one hand on your chest and the other on your belly.

3. Close your eyes and focus on your breath.

4. Now, breathe deeply through your nose. Feel your belly expand as it fills your body with life-giving oxygen.

5. If your belly doesn't expand, take a moment and try again, focusing your attention on taking a deep breath.

6. Hold your breath for a count of three, and then begin exhaling through your mouth.

7. Feel your stomach and chest return to its normal position.

8. Instead of stopping when your body is in a normal position, push your breath out, emptying your lungs completely. Aim to exhale for a count of seven.

9. Repeat these steps 4–8 for two minutes or even longer if you still feel the need to act compulsively.

CBT Exercise 8: The Alphabet Game

This CBT exercise is great for distracting your mind and effectively forcing your body to act compulsively. The best part about the alphabet game is that it can be done anywhere at any time and doesn't require you to sit or lie down.

When you're feeling anxious or engaging in compulsive behaviors, begin with the steps below.

Instructions

1. Take a deep breath.

2. Keep your eyes open and exhale slowly.

3. Notice your environment and say where you are out loud.

4. Now, begin naming things in your environment, beginning with the letter "a."

5. Give yourself five seconds to name your "a" object before moving on to the letter "b."

6. Don't worry if you cannot find an object with the corresponding letter; simply give yourself five seconds and move on.

7. Continue with steps 4 to 6, going through the entire alphabet.

CBT methods are some of the most effective ways for you to manage your OCD symptoms as a teen. It teaches you amazing self-regulation skills while helping you to reframe your thoughts and learn coping strategies to manage stress and fear responses.

Using CBT as a tool sets you up for success, as it doesn't seek to uncover your past or the cause of your thoughts. Rather, it helps you to understand that sometimes we can have completely untrue thought patterns, and this doesn't mean we're going to act on them. In fact, literally everyone on earth has cognitive distortions that can feel disturbing from time to time, and this means you're not the odd kid—you're just learning to navigate your mind.

Chapter 2:
Exposure and Response Prevention Therapy (ERP) for OCD

ERP is a form of cognitive behavioral therapy that is used in the treatment of OCD from as young as the teenage years all the way through adulthood. For disorders like OCD, exposure and response prevention therapy is incredibly useful in confronting the images, thoughts, and objects that trigger both our obsessions and our compulsions.

Now, before I continue with this chapter, I want to make it clear that there is a difference between exposure therapy and ERP. Exposure therapy is used by therapists to help people overcome their fears by exposing them to the stimulus that is causing anxiety and fear in a safe environment.

ERP, however, is the art of confronting the images, objects, thoughts, and environments that trigger us without necessarily being exposed to them and using tools to prevent our compulsive behaviors once we feel anxiety or fear.

Because of the common myth that ERP and exposure therapy are the same thing, many people never seek out treatment using this really useful form of therapy. Now, I'm not denying that confronting the things that trigger our compulsions is challenging. The reality is that without actually confronting our triggers, it's going to be very difficult to retrain our brains and learn how to manage our symptoms.

Okay, so now that you know the hard part, you're actually going to have to confront the things that make us anxious and fearful. Because of this, you may want to complete the exercises below with an adult or a safe person close by so that you resist the urge to act on your compulsions.

What You Can Expect From ERP

The goal of ERP is to help you retrain your brain to *not* act on your compulsions once they have been triggered by internal or external stimuli. In the beginning phases of doing these exercises, you may feel a bit overwhelmed, and that's okay! Always remember to be kind and non-judgmental when trying something new, and remember that it will take time for you to get the hang of it.

Before I dive into the exercises, it's important that you know all of the things you may experience when practicing ERP—some of these are not so great while others, over time, will help calm your anxiety and help you act.

- You may experience an increase in anxiety or even obsessions when you first begin these exercises. This is normal and will pass over time… Persevere, persist, and make sure you have an adult or safe person with you.

- You may find that your feelings and emotions become overwhelming in the beginning phases. A great way to overcome this is to write out a big sign that says, "I am safe; this is manageable," and make copies of this sign to paste up in the different spaces of your home.

- You will need to stop fighting your obsession as well as your anxiety, and this can be really, really difficult to do. Your emotions are designed to subside, and if you allow yourself to feel the sensations you're feeling, your mind and body will begin to calm.

- You will need to acknowledge that your thoughts and feelings, while unpleasant, cannot hurt you. Again, this can be really difficult to do, especially when your mind has trained your body to act on your compulsions for you to feel safe.

- You will begin to understand that your thoughts cannot hurt you once you feel your anxiety begin to drop. This is the prevention part of ERP.

- Over time, your mind will begin to understand that you don't need to act on your obsessions for you to be safe, and you will be able to manage your need to act. This is the prevention part of ERP.

- Finally, with time and practice, your brain will retrain itself and understand that life is a series of risks and uncertainties, most of which are not going to cause you harm.

ERP Exercises to Manage Your Obsessions and Compulsions

These exercises will not be broken into two sections like they were in the previous chapter. The reason for this is that your body's alarm system, anxiety, is designed to go through a series of processes.

These processes are experiencing a perceived threat, generating an emotional response (fear or anxiety), acting on this response to keep yourself safe, and finally, the emotions and response subsiding.

A great way to think of your OCD is as an internal fire alarm. For people who don't have OCD, this alarm goes off and lets them know that something requires their attention. It's a prompt to either protect yourself or switch the alarm off… Got it?

With OCD, this alarm goes off for the smallest things—put toast in the toaster, the alarm goes off; put supper on the stove, the alarm goes off; I have a hot shower, and you guessed it, the alarm goes off!

This is what happens with OCD; it warns you that there is a danger that doesn't exist, prompting you to take action. This alarm can be so sensitive for teens that it can communicate just about anything, including thoughts, that can set it off.

This, of course, is not ideal, and you will need to be able to find out if there really is a fire before you can switch the alarm off. The thing is that most of the things that set off the teen OCD alarm are completely false or have a very small chance of actually happening.

The compulsive behaviors are merely idle attempts to keep us safe from the alarm, not what could happen. It's the equivalent of someone lighting birthday candles on your cake, but instead of blowing them out, you douse the cake in water. ERP will help you see that birthday candles are not much of a threat, and a simple action will help rectify the situation.

Right, now that you know what ERP is and how it works, let's get to the exercises.

ERP Exercise 1: False Alarm Worksheet

The worksheet below will help you identify the thought, environmental stimulus, or object that is triggering your compulsions.

I like to color code my worksheets so that I have a visual cue of where my OCD is and how it is making me feel. For example, block 1—intrusive thought is yellow or orange; block 2—anxiety is red; block 3—action is blue; and block 4—relief is green.

You can use any colors you like that resonate with how you're feeling in the moment. Having this visual representation of how your emotions and feelings pass over time will help you work through each of the steps required to calm yourself and confront your thoughts. It's important that you acknowledge that all emotions will pass in a maximum of 90 seconds if you allow them to.

I have completed the first block for you as an example of how you can incorporate this exercise into your life.

Intrusive Thought	Anxiety	Action	Relief
Example: I am going to fail my exam.	I feel hollow in my belly; my hands are sweating, my heart is racing…	Belly breathing for 4 minutes, focusing on all of the work I have put in.	I feel better because I know that I have done the best I can.

ERP Exercise 2: Overcoming Intrusive Thoughts

For you to practice ERP properly, you must first be able to identify your intrusive thoughts. While this might sound simple, when we have OCD, these thoughts can be so persistent and intense that we believe them to be real.

Please remember that a belief is not a fact, and these thoughts are the cause of the fire alarm going off in your mind. If you look at things with a rational mind, you're not going to throw away your supper or eat ice-cold food for the remainder of your life just because the alarm isn't working the way it should.

For you to enjoy your food and eat all of the things you love, you're going to have to *accept* that cooking the food is necessary in the first place. But how are you ever going to practice acceptance if you're blaming your food and not the fire alarm?

Do you see how this all works?

Here's how to overcome your intrusive thoughts with *acceptance* and *self-love*.

1. Have a pen and paper or your mobile device with you at all times during your OCD management journey. This will ensure you've always got the most basic tools needed to note your intrusive thoughts when they occur.

2. Write down or type out your intrusive thoughts.

3. Label it for what it is by using the following sentence: "This is an *intrusive thought*." Here's an example, "I am going to trip, fall, and hurt myself if my room is not perfect—*This is an intrusive thought!*"

4. Now continue your sentence with the phrase, "This thought is *automatic*." An example of this is, "I am going to trip, fall, and hurt myself if my room is not perfect. This is an *intrusive thought!* This thought is *automatic*."

5. Here comes the tough part… Take a deep breath and allow the thought to reside in your mind. Don't try to push it away; just let it exist. You can even write out another step if you like to help you accept its existence.

6. Put your hand on your chest. Focus on your breathing and your heartbeat, taking some deep breaths in and exhaling out of your mouth.

7. Feel your heartbeat slow, and your breathing becomes more regular.

8. Take as long as you need for your mind to stop fixating on the thought and move on to something else. Usually, this takes only 3 minutes.

9. Once the intrusive thought has passed, take one more deep breath and accept that this exercise will not stop intrusive thoughts. Everyone has these types of automatic responses and thoughts; it's a normal part of being a human, and we don't need to act on them to feel safe.

I've written out an example of how I completed this exercise to help you better understand how you can move through each of these steps.

This thought is *automatic*. An example of this is, "I am going to trip, fall, and hurt myself if my room is not perfect." This is an *intrusive thought*! This thought is *automatic*. I do not have control over my thoughts, but I can control my breath. I am going to draw focus to my *breath* and *heartbeat*. Inhale… exhale… inhale… exhale… I *accept* that this thought will return because it is *automatic*. A *recurring automatic* thought doesn't *need* my attention or *action*.

ERP Exercise 3: Say Goodbye to Catastrophizing

Catastrophic thoughts, or catastrophizing, are both a big word and a big concept to try to wrap your mind around. If we simplify it, catastrophizing is merely getting stuck in the "*what ifs*" or "*shoulds.*"

People of all ages and types experience catastrophizing at one or more points in their lives, and this can lead to everything from procrastination to avoidance, lowered self-esteem, and even OCD. There is, however, a difference between OCD *what ifs* and getting stuck temporarily, and this is that OCD has us feeling like we're stuck permanently.

For other people, intrusive *what if* thoughts are relatively fleeting, and once a person realizes that the thought doesn't align with their behavior or what is going on in their life, they move on. If they believe their behavior doesn't align with their thoughts, they make small changes so that they change their narrative to *"I am."*

When we have OCD, these thoughts become stuck—we fixate on them, and ultimately we begin to participate in compulsions to help make sure the *what ifs* never come to pass. Instead of analyzing our actual behavior and pitting it against our intrusive thoughts, our brains seek to solve a problem that doesn't exist. Our final step, the *I am*, becomes filled with behaviors that we know are not really constructive, but we feel that we can temporarily fix them if we act in the moment.

Now, if you take the time to analyze your thoughts, you'll notice a lot of them begin with *what if*, and a lot of your compulsions begin with *I should*. Let's look at an OCD example.

"*What if* I fail my exam? I *should* study in all my free time! *I am* going to cut my sleep time in half so that I don't fail my exam." And the following evening, the pattern repeats because the temporary action has only served to make the situation worse because you're tired and functioning through brain fog. The brain fog means you cannot recall what you have learned, and the cycle begins again: "*What if* I fail my exam?..."

Do you see how catastrophizing works?

Now let's look at the same example, reframed.

> *What if* I fail my exam? I *have* studied to the best of my ability. *I am* going to take an hour tonight to review my work so that I can put my mind at ease.

Like all of the other exercises in this book, you're going to need to identify when you are catastrophizing so that you can find constructive solutions. The good news is that most of the time, these thoughts are easy to identify because they begin with *what if* and contain an *I should* to drive the compulsion.

When using the table below, you're not only uncovering your catastrophic thoughts, but you're also able to challenge them and put into action a positive, constructive plan to give you the best shot at a good outcome.

My *what if* thought is:

What is the cause of my *what if* thought? What am I worried about?

How likely is it that *this* will happen? (Make sure to provide evidence and facts to support this step):

What is the *worst* that can happen? (Provide evidence to support this step?):

What is the *best* that can happen?
What *constructive* behaviors can I do to encourage the *best* outcome? (Provide evidence to support this step):
How will these *constructive* behaviors improve my well-being? (Provide evidence to support this step):

If you like, you can put all of these steps into one or two sentences so that you can print it out and paste it up as a reminder or focus point when you're feeling anxiety or the need to act compulsively.

ERP Exercise 4: Rating Your Anxiety Triggers

Sometimes, no matter what we do, our body goes into a state of anxiety. This anxiety can feel like a low-level buzz that hangs around all day and exhausts us, or it can escalate to full panic and compulsive behavior.

Knowing the things that trigger you and how severe these things are can help you not only manage your anxiety and compulsion symptoms but also begin practicing some great coping behaviors.

If you don't know what these coping behaviors are, don't worry; they will be covered in Chapter 5. For now, let's look at some common anxiety triggers for teenagers so that you can identify which ones affect you and rate them appropriately.

I have left some blank spaces for you to fill in your own unique anxieties:

Anxiety	Rating 1 to 10
I expect myself to be perfect	
I feel out of control	
I don't want to disappoint my family	
I'm scared I won't be accepted by my friends	
I fear peer pressure	
I am scared of alcohol and drugs	
I am scared to stand out	
I worry about never being successful	
The world is a scary place	

Once you have identified your triggers and rated them from 1 to 10, it's important that you take the time to identify the ones that cause you the most anxiety. Anything above a 5 is problematic, and anything over a 7 needs your attention.

Once you begin to feel your anxiety calm and can manage your compulsions for groups 7 and above, you can begin to address your 5 and 6 lists. All of the fears on your list can be improved upon and made manageable by completing the exercises in the previous chapters as well as using the techniques listed in Chapter 6.

ERP Exercise 5: Qualifying the Positive

Having OCD means, we can often spend a lot of time convincing ourselves that the positive evidence is just not true. We give all of our attention to the negative, and when we do this, we form an all-or-nothing thinking pattern.

As you know, cognitive distortions and intrusive thoughts are almost always automatic, and when we reinforce these thoughts by disqualifying the positive, we reinforce all of the negative things that *could* happen to us that *are* our own fault and which we *should* have prevented.

Living in a world where we're taking personal responsibility for things that are often completely out of our control begins to cause anxiety because we are training our brain to believe the worst is going to happen every time we don't act. And, when our brain believes danger is imminent, it enters a state of fight or flight, raising our anxiety levels and compelling us to act immediately so that we can remain safe.

But when we're stuck in a cycle of disqualifying the positive, it can be difficult to spot, especially when we pay more attention to all of the things that can go wrong in any situation. Look at the scenario below and see if you can spot the disqualification.

> I should tear this assignment up and begin over. All of the feedback I got was to improve certain areas! It doesn't matter that some of the feedback was positive; this assignment is trash!

Now, if you examine the statement above, what clues are being given that identify this thought as a cognitive distortion, all-or-nothing thinking, and catastrophizing?

- Should—catastrophizing

- Most—all-or-nothing thinking

- Start over–compulsion

- All of the feedback—cognitive distortion and all-or-nothing thinking

- Trash—all-or-nothing thinking

- It doesn't matter that some feedback was positive—disqualifying the positive

When I unravel this scenario for you, does it become easier to see how quickly cognitive distortions can become compulsions that we justify by disqualifying the positive?

So how do you begin qualifying the positive to break the cycle of all-or-nothing thinking and cognitive distortions? You need to begin training your brain to qualify the positive by turning its behavior back on itself and disqualifying the distortion.

Using the worksheet below, I'd like you to think of a scenario in which you behaved compulsively. Place this scenario in the relevant column and follow the steps to help you begin qualifying the positive. You can use this exercise as many times as you like to retrain your brain and focus on the positive.

Exercise Key

ANT: all-or-nothing thinking

FTC: fortune-telling or catastrophizing

DP: disqualifying the positive

ER: emotional response

L: labeling

MR: mind reading

SS: should statements

UT: unhelpful thoughts

The situation:

Automatic thoughts:	Thought type: ANT, FTC, DP, ER, and so on.

Emotions I feel:
- Anxious
- Nervous
- Irritated
- Embarrassed
- Ashamed
- Other

- Frustrated
- Angry
- Hateful
- Sad
- Guilty

Facts that qualify as positive:

Positive Outcome:	Positive Actions to Take:

Once you have completed this worksheet, you can begin to formulate positive action plans and goals. And if you're not sure how to set goals or use feedback, don't worry; I've got you covered in later chapters.

ERP may sound like a really scary thing to do, and I'm not denying that at some point during these exercises, you may begin to feel overwhelmed. What is important is that you treat yourself with love and compassion as you begin to uncover your cognitive distortions and face them head-on.

With patience and practice, you will begin to become a master of not only identifying these thoughts but also acknowledging them for what they are—the fleeting thoughts that sometimes reside in your mind.

Chapter 3:
Psychodynamic Therapy

For teens with OCD, psychodynamic therapy can be extremely useful in understanding the reasons our compulsions are triggered. In essence, it provides us with the *why* behind our thoughts and gives valuable insight into the processes and emotions that may be contributing to our thoughts and behaviors.

While traditional psychodynamic therapy focuses quite heavily on past experiences that may have contributed to our behaviors, this section is *not* going to drag up our pasts. Instead, we're going to focus on exercises that help us identify our unconscious processes, explore our defense mechanisms or compulsions, discover how we may be projecting our feelings and beliefs, and begin to discover the value of self-reflection and insight.

Before you begin with the exercises below, I'd like you to know that psychodynamic therapy is a long-term thing, and you're going to have to put in some effort to help you find those deep-rooted thought patterns that are driving your behaviors.

Having said that, I know that you have the tenacity and motivation to not only get through these exercises but to repeat them so that you can reap the benefits of your OCD management journey.

ERP Exercises to Help Manage Your Obsessions and Compulsions

As a teen with OCD, your quality of life can be greatly affected by your compulsions, and your mental well-being suffers because of the intense, intrusive thoughts you have. Psychodynamic Therapy is a very useful tool that doesn't use typical techniques for treating OCD.

Now, the reason I say these techniques are not the first-line treatment for OCD is that they're meant to be used together with other tools like CBT. But that's not to say that psychodynamic therapy is not a necessary step in managing your techniques because it focuses on exploring the underlying dynamics that are at the root of both your thoughts and behaviors.

In addition, these tools help you to address any issues that may be co-occurring, like an event in your life that isn't quite resolved, as well as your anxiety and any feelings of sadness or depression you may be having.

When doing these exercises, don't be surprised if your rituals are revealed to be symbolic in some way or are connected to what you do to soothe yourself when something traumatic or bad happens in your life.

Most importantly, psychodynamic therapy helps you become self-aware, building insight into why you may be having the thoughts you're having. When used with the other tools in this book, the exercises in this chapter will help you enhance your coping mechanisms. This means you should *not* do these exercises as a stand-alone but rather as an added bonus that will help you supercharge your OCD management tools.

Psychodynamic Exercise 1: Free Association

This tool is designed to help you express how you're feeling, thinking, and any other associations without any judgment or initial analysis. When completing this tool, it's important that you are in a calm space, so if you're feeling a bit anxious, try to do some of the breathing or meditation exercises in this book.

I'd like you to go into this exercise without expectations… and, if you're battling to do that, just tell yourself there is no point to this exercise at all.

1. Have this exercise ready so that you can fill it in digitally.

2. Find a quiet spot where you can sit comfortably.

3. Remind yourself that you are safe.

4. When you are ready, fill in the blocks below.

5. Each of these blocks should continue from the other. I have filled in the first section as an example for you.

My thought is:	When I think about this, I feel:	When I think about this, I want to:	Why do I believe I feel this way:
Nobody really likes me.	Scared, lonely, and ashamed.	Isolate myself from everyone to prevent myself from getting hurt.	Because I was psychologically bullied in elementary school.

Remember that this exercise is a judgment-free zone. If you find yourself judging yourself, stop the exercise, take a break, and come back to it later. Once you have completed these blocks, take a look at what you have written, reading it out loud.

Do you see a pattern emerging?

Write this pattern down and apply it to the next exercise.

Psychodynamic Exercise 2: The Five Whys

This exercise is designed to help your brain begin to solve problems in a constructive way. A lot of the time, we try to tackle problems based on how we are feeling or thinking rather than understanding the *why* behind the issue at hand.

The problem with not knowing the *why* is that we never find out what is causing us to repeat our behaviors, and the problem comes back over and over again because we're applying the same solution as before.

We need to be able to define the problem specifically so that we can investigate it further and apply the right solution to what we're facing. But people often don't think this way, and instead of finding out *why* something has happened, they jump to a conclusion or brush over the cause, hoping for a quick fix. Now, if this is you, please don't feel bad—literally, everyone has experienced this kind of problem-solving issue at least once in their life.

Let me give you an example.

You wake up one morning and get to your car, only to find the battery is dead. Instead of finding out why, you come up with a solution; Change the battery or have roadside assistance jumpstart your car.

Once you're at school, you park your car, only to come back later and find the battery dead. At this point, you may ask yourself *why*, but most people won't go beyond this. The five whys help you to go beyond this instant solution, as well as the first *why*, to help you uncover the real underlying issues you are facing.

Using the pattern, you identified in the exercise before this, use the steps below to uncover the real reason you may be experiencing your thoughts. An example is provided in the first set of five questions, and a second set of five questions is provided for you to duplicate and fill in.

1. **Define the problem**: I am lonely because I think others don't like me.

2. **Why did this problem occur?** I was bullied in elementary school.

3. **Formulate the second reason based on the first answer. Why?** Was I bullied in elementary school? My parents moved, and I was shy when I attended my new school.

4. **Formulate the third reason based on the second answer. Why?** Was I shy? My old friends said they would keep in touch, but they didn't. I was shy because I was afraid my new friends would abandon me too.

5. **Formulate the fourth why based on the third answer. Why?** Did they not contact me? My parents said our number had changed and my friends didn't know.

6. **Formulate the fifth why based on the fourth answer or conclude**: If my friends didn't know how to contact me, they didn't really abandon me. I can conclude that I feel lonely because I lack confidence in forming new connections. The solution to this problem is to work on my self-esteem.

If you look at the example above, you can see that the real problem is not being bullied, even if it appears to be on the surface. The real issue stems from a fear of being abandoned and low self-esteem.

Now it's your turn. Fill in the answers below so that you can uncover the real problem as well as the proper solution to it:

1. Define the problem

2. Why did this problem occur

3. Formulate the second why based on the first answer–why

4. Formulate the third why based on the second answer–why

5. Formulate the fourth why based on the third answer–why

6. Formulate the fifth why based on the fourth answer, or conclude

Once you have uncovered the deeper cause of what you're facing, you can begin to apply the proper tools and techniques to help solve the issue. In the example provided, the teen could practice self-care routines, work within their strengths while improving on their weaknesses, or join a club surrounding their interests so that new friendships can be formed.

Psychodynamic Exercise 3: The Empty Chair

This exercise is designed to help you uncover and resolve the feelings and thoughts you may have that you have repressed for whatever reason. As teens, we often feel like we're not heard or that if we speak about the things that have upset us, it will cause conflict we would rather not engage in.

If this is you, I'd like you to know that it's not unusual for teens to bottle up their feelings or not know how to communicate what they're feeling accurately. Your brain simply isn't mature enough yet to be able to formulate the words you need, especially when you're feeling emotional, hurt, or upset.

And when we know that the words, we need are not going to be adequate to describe how we feel, we can begin to feel guilt, shame, or even frustration, compounding the issue at hand. Over time, repressed emotions can build up and spill over, and we can ruminate, playing the situation over and over again in our heads.

The empty chair exercise allows you to express how you're feeling without fear or judgment because the other person or people are not present. Over time, it teaches you how to communicate your feelings properly, allowing you to build the confidence needed to deal with conflict and express your thoughts.

You can set up a space in your room to complete this exercise or use the worksheet prompts below to begin practicing the empty chair as a thought or emotion is noticed:

Instructions

1. Set up your space first. Place two chairs facing each other. One chair is for you, and the other will remain empty.

2. Alternatively, open your worksheet so that you can follow the prompts and write down your experience when you can, set up your space, and read the answers on your worksheet out loud.

3. Choose a person, thought, or image that needs to be addressed. This can be anyone in the past or present, your inner critic, your thoughts, or even an aspect of your personality you are conflicting with.

4. Close your eyes and imagine this person sitting in an empty chair.

5. If you're using this worksheet to revisit at a later stage, imagine the person or image in front of you, wherever you are.

6. Bring as many details as possible into your imagery. Try to recreate the person's clothes, the environment you were in, how things smelled, what you were hearing, and so on.

7. If you're dealing with an image, inner critic, or aspect of your personality, assign each of these characteristics and employ as many of your senses as you possibly can.

8. Using the prompts below, begin expressing how you feel, what your thoughts are, and so on.

Prompt 1: Scenario	
Prompt 2: I felt	
Prompt 3: The reason	
Prompt 4: My perspective	
Prompt 5: It's important	
Prompt 6: I need	

Here is a completed example to help guide you:

I am imagining my eldest sister. She was wearing a gray sweatshirt and black sweatpants. She was on her bed, using her phone. Music was playing, and the room smelled like her perfume. Her hair was in a bun, and she seemed to be interested in the text conversation on her phone.

Prompt 1: Scenario	I came into your room to tell you I made the football team. I was feeling proud and excited, and I wanted to share my experience with you. I greeted you and told you about my success. I didn't get the experience I expected, as you didn't even lift your head and continued to text. You said well done and continued with what you were doing. I was left hanging in silence, and I left your room.
Prompt 2: I felt	I felt completely dismissed as if you didn't care. It felt like you were more interested in whatever was going on behind your screen. This made me feel like I don't even exist to you or that you don't care about what is going on in my life. I was sad, a little angry, and I didn't feel like sharing this experience or any other with anyone else.
Prompt 3: The reason	The reason I wanted to share my experience with you is that I value your opinion and would like your praise and validation.
Prompt 4: My perspective	My perspective is that everyone and everything is more important than I am when it comes to you. I will never be interesting enough for you to pay the same attention to me as you do to other things.
Prompt 5: It's important	It's important to me that you pay attention to me because I want to feel loved, accepted, and appreciated by you. I believe that with your validation, I have a better chance of succeeding.
Prompt 6: I need	I need you to show me love and appreciation and to let me know you are proud of me.

Once you have expressed your perspective and how you felt, it's time to reverse roles and try to see this scenario from the other person's perspective.

Here's the example from above from the other person's perspective:

Prompt 1: Scenario	You came into my room without knocking and said hi. You didn't give me a chance to say hi back before you started talking. I understand you were excited, but I was in the middle of a conversation. By the time I was done typing the sentence, you had left.
Prompt 2: I felt	I felt disrespected because you came into my space without knocking and dismissed what I was doing to tell me your news. I feel that if you had given me a chance to finish what I was doing, we could have had a conversation. I felt angry when you left.
Prompt 3: The reason	The reason I felt disrespected is that you have an expectation for privacy and respect but often don't afford other people the same.
Prompt 4: My perspective	My perspective is that if you slowed down and allowed me the chance to finish what I was doing or communicated that you had something exciting to share, things would have gone a lot better.
Prompt 5: It's important	It's important to me that you respect my privacy and communicate your intentions to me before you begin talking to me.
Prompt 6: I need	I need you to know that I do love and appreciate you and that, with the right steps taken, we can share things a lot easier and without conflict.

Once you have completed this step, you will need to take some time to reflect on what you have learned and begin to integrate it into your daily practices. Ask yourself if it feels like this conversation has been resolved for you and take the time to consider how you're feeling now that you have had a chance to express yourself and see things from the other person's perspective.

Psychodynamic Exercise 4: Projection and Transference Detector

Okay, so this is a difficult concept to understand for most adults, especially because people don't like to admit that they may be causing some of their own suffering and pain.

Way back when psychology was in its birth phase, psychologists noted that sometimes their patients would develop strong feelings or direct their inner thoughts and feelings directly to the therapist.

Treating people differently because we feel something for someone else is called transference, and taking our feelings and attitude out on other people because of something internal we're feeling is called projection.

There are a number of reasons we can end up both transferring and projecting our feelings and perceptions onto others, but the most common of these reasons is not processing our emotions adequately or wanting someone to save us from our inner anxieties.

Everyone has been subject to transference or projection at some point in their lives. Think about it... Maybe one of your parents came home after a hard day at work and snapped at you when you didn't do anything wrong. This is a projection.

Or, you may be feeling really low and sad, and you begin to think that your best friend is depressed, insisting they get help; this is transference.

It's really important that you can identify instances in your own life where you may be transferring or projecting how you feel because you need to be able to take ownership of your OCD in order to manage it.

This doesn't mean you are to blame for your OCD—quite the opposite!—but you do need to acknowledge that you have a choice in managing your symptoms, and the only way to do that is to take ownership of your behaviors without transferring them or projecting them on others.

Fill in the worksheet below to help you identify your transference or projection and uncover what internal issues you may need to resolve to better manage your OCD symptoms.

Scenario	T/P	Thought	Reframe
My best friend is depressed and needs help.	Projection and Transference.	I am feeling really sad lately, and I don't know why.	I am depressed and need help. I will speak to an adult.

Psychodynamic therapy is a very useful tool you can use to manage your symptoms when it is used with other forms of therapeutic exercise. It's important that you explore the reasons why you are feeling the way you are so that you can work on the real issues at hand rather than on the surface presentations of these internal thoughts and feelings.

With practice and time, you will begin to learn to identify how you are feeling as well as how to communicate these feelings and thoughts in a way that encourages healing.

Chapter 4:
Acceptance and Commitment Therapy (ACT)

While ACT wasn't always the first line of treatment for OCD, it has gained popularity over the last few years as one of the main tools people use to manage their symptoms. For teens, ACT is particularly exciting because it teaches us in the early phases of our lives to openly experience our feelings, the sensations in our bodies, and our thoughts.

Once we can learn to accept our experiences without judgment and with empathy, we begin to become less impacted by them, and this is great news because we can begin to move toward our goals without the obstacles OCD places in front of us.

I don't want to sugarcoat life—it can be extremely challenging at times, and when we throw OCD into the mix, we can sometimes feel like we're stuck in a mess of one obsessive thought after the next as we face the difficulties life throws at us.

Rejection, failure, emotional and physical pain, loss, and disappointment are all aspects of life that we will need to face so that we can see the joys in other areas of this amazing journey we're on.

When we have OCD, however, it can feel almost impossible to find anything amazing as our mind tries to warn us about all of the things that *could* go wrong instead of showing us all of the things that are *more* likely to go right. We can become stuck, ruminating on our past as confirmation that things do go wrong, and this is where ACT can help.

As a therapeutic practice, ACT shows us that our thoughts and feelings are not important if we don't pay attention to them and practice acceptance while committing to our healing. We can begin to navigate what thoughts are actually important and what we can allow to just pass through space and time.

In other words, instead of trying to avoid your thoughts, you're going to learn how to become flexible in your thinking and identify what you need to pay attention to. By reducing your internal struggle with your thoughts, you will start to understand that there is no way to eliminate what you think or the experiences you've had. But you do have the power to manage what is happening in your life right now in a constructive way.

ACT Exercise 1: Thought Diffuser

A hallmark trait of OCD is that our thoughts consume a lot of our time and attention. This can feel incredibly distressing, and we can begin to fixate on what behaviors will ease our internal strife.

When we do this, it's called "being fused with thoughts," and it can be incredibly upsetting and frustrating, causing feelings of anxiety, panic, and even the need to control our environment.

Thought diffusion provides you with the tools to get out of this trap your mind has created for you by shifting your focus from what the thought is—the content—and placing your attention on the processes of your thoughts.

What happens when we shift focus is that the mind begins to calm as it shifts out of its emotional state and into its rational one. This leads to greater mental clarity and a balanced perspective on what is going on in your life. The worksheet below provides you with powerful and sometimes fun tools that are specifically designed to help you shift your brain from irrational to rational.

Read each of the instructions in each block and then either act out or use the provided block to help shift your mindset within a matter of minutes.

Technique	Writing Block
Head in the clouds: Take a moment to close your eyes and imagine your head is surrounded by clouds. Watch the clouds floating by, weightless and wispy. Now, imagine taking your thoughts and placing it on the cloud. Give this thought a name or an image. Take the time to say goodbye to this thought and watch it float away.	
Impersonate a cartoon: When a thought is ruminating and plaguing you, take a moment to think of a cartoon character with a silly voice. Capture their voice in your mind, and then say your thoughts in the cartoon's voice. Add sarcasm and humor as you say your thoughts out loud and allow yourself to laugh.	
Shut it down: When you have more than one thought ruminating in your mind, it can feel like a busy place—somewhat like a web browser with too many pages open. Take a moment to imagine your mind in this web browser. Address each thought by opening the page, acknowledging you don't need it, and finally hitting the X on the top right corner of the page, shutting it down.	

I'm having: When a thought is really disturbing, it's a good idea to name it and distance yourself from it so that it becomes impersonal. This can be done by placing the phrase "I'm having" in front of your named thought.	
Place it in a box: When a space is cluttered, it can feel overwhelming, and placing things we don't need in a box to be donated can help free up space and reduce anxiety. The same is true for your mind. Take a moment to imagine your mind as a big room filled with clutter. Now imagine that there is a large box. Place each unhelpful thought in your mind in this box. Finally, close the box up and imagine it being carried away.	

Using the empty spaces in the worksheet above is not a necessity but will help you identify which thoughts you're going to address during your visualization exercises. Any thoughts that are persistent or recur a lot of the time can be addressed using the CBT or ERP exercises in this book.

ACT Exercise 2: Vitality Versus Suffering Evaluation

Our obsessive thoughts can overtake our minds, causing us to feel like our lives are an endless loop of suffering and overwhelm. And when we try to soothe ourselves with compulsive behaviors, we can often lose time, experience frustration, and even cause ourselves physical pain.

Life is a series of choices that we make either consciously or subconsciously, and OCD can sometimes rob us of these choices as our body acts on a subconscious level in an attempt to stop the obsessive thoughts we are having.

In practicing the exercises in previous chapters, we can begin to identify these negative thoughts as well as the reasons we may have begun trying to deal with them in some not-so-great ways.

Here's the thing about the choices we need to make in our lives: They can lead to vitality or suffering, and this means we need to bring our subconscious thoughts to the conscious so that we can find out what it is that is causing us suffering in the first place.

Now, before you begin with this exercise, I'd like to explain that suffering doesn't mean some awful, cataclysmic state of being. It could be the low hum of chronic anxiety, the feeling that we need to do certain things to soothe ourselves, or even paying attention to the negative thoughts in our minds.

Suffering, like joy, happens on a scale, and something that may feel like a small irritation to you may be something that is causing someone else enormous amounts of discomfort. And that is why this worksheet is so important—it identifies what is causing *you* suffering as well as what brings you vitality in your life.

Using the prompts in the table below, fill in the thoughts that cause you to feel terrible and the ones that make you feel great. This can be done the moment you experience these thoughts, or it can be completed in a quiet, reflective moment while you are evaluating your day.

Remember to use the exercise below this one to clarify whether or not your negative thoughts align with your values so that you can dispel the lingering, intense thoughts that cause you suffering.

Thought, feeling, compulsion, memory, or sensation I am experiencing.	What behavior or action did I take that caused me suffering (restricted, drained, or hurt me)?	What behavior or action did I take that caused me vitality (enriched, made me happy, helped me feel like it was manageable)?

ACT Exercise 3: Clarifying Your Values

A lot of the time, our intrusive OCD thoughts are completely the opposite of our values in life. We know that we are not the people our thoughts say we are, but without clarifying our values, it can become difficult to put our thoughts to rest.

The worksheet below is designed as a framework that allows you to explore and reflect upon your personal values so that you can see how your thoughts don't line up with your values.

It's important that you go down the list of values, ascertaining your values in all of the different aspects of your life. If one of these blocks doesn't apply to you yet, like a career, then you can skip over it.

Here are the categories:

- **Career**: What career would you love to have? What does your ideal organization look like? What qualities would you like to develop to be an asset to your ideal company? What type of coworker would you like to be?

- **Family relationships**: What kind of relationship would you like with your parents? Do you have siblings? What relationship would you like to have with your siblings? What behaviors do you think you could model to form these relationships?

- **Friendships**: What kind of people would you like to surround yourself with? What do you consider to be the most important part of friendship? What would you like your friends to see about you as a person?

- **Health and physical wellness**: What do you define as being fit and healthy? What are your goals for your health and wellness? How important is your mental health when considering your overall well-being? What does self-care look like to you?

- **Leisure and fun**: What activities do you love doing? If money was no object, how would you enjoy your downtime? What do you find interesting, exciting, and relaxing?

- **Personal development**: What aspects of your personal development would you like to give focus to? How do you think you could develop your skills so that you can succeed in life? What does success look like to you?

- **Romantic relationships**: What would you like in a life partner, or what would your ideal relationship look like? What behavior do you want to project to attract a life partner?

- **Social and environmental responsibility**: What do you define as a community? How would you like to fit into a community? What does this community look like? How important is the environment to you? What volunteer work could you do to help the environment or your community?

- **Spirituality**: How do you define spirituality? What aspects of your spirituality do you believe need addressing? What are your personal beliefs? How do you feel that you can strengthen your spirituality?

Now that you know what categories and questions you can answer to help align your values with your thoughts and behaviors, feel free to use the table below to write down notes and set goals to align your values with your thoughts.

Career		
Family relationships		

Friendships		
Health and physical wellness		
Leisure and fun		
Personal development		
Romantic relationships		

Social and environmental responsibility		
Spirituality		
Notes:		

ACT Exercise 4: Observation

Teens can have extremely full lives. Between school, homework, studies, extracurricular activities, our friends, and home and family responsibilities, we can sometimes forget to check in with ourselves.

We pay attention and notice all of the things around us, making sure that we don't missteps. And it's not that these people and tasks don't require our attention; it's just that we are *important* too.

Then there is the infinite number of strangers and stimuli we are exposed to every day that we may or may not be consciously aware of, and our brains take all of this in, filling the things we don't need right now into our subconscious.

Not being mindful and grounded in the present can sometimes mean our brain can become confused, pulling from this subconscious resource bin and presenting other people's realities as our own.

This exercise is designed to help you remain present and in the moment and to become more aware of your environment so that your conscious mind can begin to let your subconscious mind know what your reality is and what is someone else's.

It also teaches you to become observant of yourself and how you are feeling in the moment, drawing attention to the moments when you're feeling calm, unpressured, and content with life.

You will need to spend an entire hour completing this exercise in a public place like a coffee shop or local park, so make sure you're setting aside a time when you will not be rushed or disturbed.

Always remember to let an adult know where you're going and what you're doing so that you remain safe. Do *not* go to an isolated spot, as this is against the purpose of the exercise and may make you feel like you're in danger.

Instructions

1. Choose your public space. This could be a mall food court, coffee shop, park, or restaurant.

2. Bring a notebook with you as well as a pen with a backup pen.

3. Have your phone with you, and make sure you let people know where you are and how long you will be gone. Ask them not to disturb you while you're exercising.

4. Travel to your destination, settle down and place your tools (your journal, pens, and phone) in front of you.

5. Order something if you like, but only begin your exercise once your food or drink has arrived.

6. Set your phone for one hour, and then place it face down on the table in front of you so that notifications don't disturb you. If your phone has the function of being placed on silent or airplane mode, but your alarm will still go off, even better!

7. Begin to observe the people around you and write down these observations in your journal. Allow your mind to muse about their lives, and when something comes up in your mind, write it down. Make sure you're spending most of your time observing, though—this is not a writing exercise; it's an observation exercise.

8. Once you have gotten the hang of observing the people around you and passing by, begin to observe yourself. Write down how you're feeling and if you have any self-observations. Make sure that you are not censoring your feelings or your observations.

9. Move your attention to your surroundings, employing your five senses to take in your environment. Write down your observations and how your environment feels about you.

10. Try to keep your mind in a judgment-free zone and look at your surroundings with curiosity. The point is to stay in the moment and discover the world without fear or judgment.

11. If your mind begins to wander or if you begin to find that you're judging yourself or others, write down this phrase, read it over, take a deep breath,

and carry on with your exercise: "I am here for an hour to discover the simple truths in life and observe my biases."

12. When your hour is up, put your pen down, pack away your journal, and carry on with whatever tasks you need to do next.

13. You can return to your journal no earlier than a day later to begin analyzing patterns in your thoughts as well as what stimuli triggered feelings of anxiety, stress, joy, contentment, or even calm.

14. Using the prompts in the table below, you will gain a deeper insight into how you are viewing the world and can work toward not only living in the present but also freeing yourself from judgment and cognitive distortion.

15. Make sure to use the CBT and ERP exercises above to help you challenge your distortions and uncover the facts.

Prompt	Answer
Am I always honest about how I feel?	
How do I feel about this exercise now?	
What were the things that made me feel negative emotions?	
What were the things that made me feel positive emotions?	
What were some things that made me jump to conclusions?	
How did I react to my surroundings and people?	
How did it feel to observe others and	

my environment?	
How did it feel to observe myself?	
What distortions did I uncover?	
What patterns of thought did I uncover?	
What made me feel most comfortable about my environment?	
What makes me most uncomfortable about my environment?	
Was there anything or anyone that I judged too harshly?	
How do I feel right now after answering these questions?	

Try to do this exercise every second week, but if you can't, it should be done at least once a month. Over time, you will notice that it becomes easier to observe your environment and yourself without judgment. You will begin to pay attention to the things that make you feel calm and will begin to focus on these things rather than the perceptions you have of threats.

ACT Exercise 5: Committed Action

One of the harshest realities we will ever face in life is that nothing is going to change if we don't put in the work to change it.

But, as a teen with OCD, this is something you're probably very aware of, and it is part of the reason that you feel such deep levels of frustration and despair when your obsessions and compulsions take over.

ACT wouldn't be helpful to us if we didn't commit to pursuing the management of our symptoms by setting goals and working toward these goals every day. With a clear plan and roadmap in place, it is easier for us to commit to our continuous improvement by taking action.

One thing I'd like to make absolutely clear when embarking upon your self-development journey and while setting goals is that you're *absolutely* allowed to love yourself exactly where you are in your journey.

Wanting to improve and develop in life doesn't mean there is something *wrong* with you that needs to be fixed. It simply means you love and *respect* yourself enough to be the best possible version of yourself.

With that being said, let's get started with the exercise. Using the table below, fill in your commitment in the form of your goals, the obstacles you may face, the solutions to these obstacles, and the milestones or steps you will take to achieve your goals.

I will fill in the first line as an example of how the exercise should be completed:

Commitment	Possible Obstacles	Possible Solutions	Milestones/Steps
I commit to completing one exercise in this book daily.	My studies and homework may take up my time.	Create a manageable schedule and ask for help.	-Create timetable -Set a reminder -Complete exercise -Reflect

ACT is an incredibly powerful tool for learning to love yourself where you are in your journey while still trying to improve your life and manage your symptoms.

As a teen, you already have so much external pressure to deal with, and ACT will help you balance this external pressure as well as manage the internal pressure you may be feeling.

With commitment, tenacity, and curiosity, you can begin to unravel your biases, learn to accept your thoughts for what they are—sometimes they are nonsensical—and gain a deeper understanding of what should be paid attention to and what can just be placed on a cloud to float away.

Chapter 5:
Mindfulness-Based Cognitive Therapy (MBCT)

Imagine combining the elements of CBT and mindfulness to create a powerful tool that helps us remember to live in the moment while still teaching us the behaviors necessary to identify our cognitive distortions. This is what MBCT is, and it has become one of the most useful forms of therapy used in the treatment of OCD as well as stress, anxiety, and depression.

When practicing MBCT techniques, you will begin to understand how getting caught up in patterns of negative thinking can often be the primary cause of the distress you feel. Through mindfulness and paying attention to what is happening in the moment while using openness and curiosity, you can begin to unravel the web of thoughts that are holding you back.

MBCT is a multifaceted approach to treating our symptoms, and this means there are different elements of the practice that need to be honed for it to become your own personal superpower in remaining calm and grounded.

These components include mindfulness training, cognitive restructuring, relapse awareness, acceptance, and self-compassion. Now, you'll notice that we have already covered some of these aspects, including a little bit of mindfulness, a whole lot of restructuring and awareness, and just a dash of acceptance. As you can see, MCBT encompasses all of the most powerful facets of other therapies, creating one formidable force against the symptoms of OCD.

MBCT Exercises for OCD

Before you throw your hands in the air and say, "How could I possibly know more than I already do about these techniques?!" The aim is not to teach you more tools, but how to combine the tools you have already learned so that you can benefit from combined therapy techniques.

We will begin this chapter by understanding what it means for you to set proper goals for your mental health and manage your OCD so that you get the most out of the exercises provided to you. Once you know what your goals are, you can create your own personal schedule for doing these exercises.

Added to this, I'll help you ask for feedback and accept it without feeling like it's a personal attack or that you're not good enough. Finally, we'll move on to some dynamic mindfulness exercises that you can use to help yourself remain calm while completing the exercises in this book.

MBCT Exercise 1: Goal Setting

Setting goals is really important in life because, without them, we don't have a clear direction or a plan for what we want to achieve and how we will achieve it. When we have OCD, goal setting can be daunting, and we can often feel like we let ourselves down because our obsessions and compulsions rob us of our time and energy.

Setting goals for your mental health will help you know what it is that you would like to achieve by doing these exercises. So, what's the difference between regular goal setting and OCD goal setting, and how will this exercise ensure you don't feel overwhelmed by your healing process?

For starters, there is no time limit to your recovery! Everyone's journey to great mental health is unique, and that means it doesn't matter how long it takes to achieve your goals. That doesn't mean you can slack off and not do your exercises, but it does mean you will not measure your progress.

Instead, you will ask others for feedback on your progress and learn to quietly reflect on how far you have come in your journey. Okay… with that out of the way, let's break down how you will set your goals. I will supply you with a table that you can use to help set your goals and monitor your progress. Always remember to celebrate your successes and victories, no matter how small they may seem.

Every new step forward toward positivity is a win!

Instructions

1. Be specific about what aspect of your OCD you would like to focus on. It's not enough to say you want to manage your OCD as a whole. Being specific means identifying the areas of your life that are most overwhelming and choosing to work on these aspects first.

2. Be realistic about what you want to achieve. You need to be clear and concise about your goal and how you would like to achieve it. Your goal should be measurable so that you can track your progress.

3. Create milestones that will break the bigger picture into smaller, more achievable actions you can take every day toward your positive progress. For example, you could commit to doing one exercise per day and institute mindfulness or meditation for just 15 minutes as an extra exercise. Milestones make goals manageable and remove the overwhelming feelings you can sometimes feel when looking at all of the steps needed to achieve a goal.

4. Find out why your goal is meaningful to you. This could be something you're working toward, like attending prom without anxiety or simply living a more peaceful life. Making a goal meaningful will ensure you are more motivated to do what needs to be done, even on days when you're feeling low.

5. Transfer your goals to an action plan. You can use the worksheet below as a simple template for what your action plan will look like.

6. Tick off each milestone so that you have visual confirmation of how much progress you're making and so that you can see just how capable you are of managing your OCD symptoms.

7. Learn to be agile because agility will keep you from slipping into perfectionism. Nothing in life ever goes according to plan, and being agile will ensure you default to acceptance and regrouping rather than anxiety and panic.

8. Ask for feedback often and learn to accept it. Don't worry; the next exercise will show you how.

9. Celebrate your achievements because you deserve acknowledgment for your success and achievements.

10. Love yourself! You've gone through a lot, teen, and you deserve to be loved, so love yourself during your journey.

My goal is	
This goal is realistic because	
My goal milestones are	
This goal is meaningful because	
I will achieve this goal by	
I celebrate myself because	
I love myself because	

An action plan could look like this:

- I will achieve my goal of going to prom without feeling anxious by identifying my cognitive distortions and learning to accept them as fleeting thoughts.

- This can be done by completing the cognitive distortion exercises daily and by doing 15 minutes of mindfulness meditation every day.

- I will complete my observation exercise twice a month so that I can learn to observe my surroundings without feeling overwhelmed or anxious about what is happening around me.

- I will ask for feedback twice a week and celebrate the progress I have made by spoiling myself with my favorite meal.

As you can see, when you break down your goals in this way, it becomes much easier to achieve them. Remember, your mental health is not a race; it's a slow marathon that requires you to pace yourself and celebrate each milestone you pass.

MBCT Exercise 2: Accepting Feedback

Before you begin with this exercise, I would like you to know that it is absolutely normal for you to not want to receive feedback. This is especially true if this feedback is not particularly great, but feedback is important for your growth and development. The timing of the feedback can also make a difference in how open we are to hear what others have to say, and let's face it; no one likes unsolicited advice or opinions.

You do, however, need to be open to receiving feedback, especially as you begin your journey to managing your OCD. The reason for this is that the OCD inner critic is often extremely harsh and will do everything in its power to convince you that you're making no progress at all or that you're not capable of making progress.

Here's the issue with a persistent inner critic: Until you've learned how to properly and effectively challenge the cognitive distortions you're having and can assertively put that inner critic into the time-out corner of your mind, you're going to need help.

This brings me to the next critical feedback point. You will need to ask for feedback from multiple trusted people in your life who can give you a wise outlook on what they believe you're improving in and what needs improvement.

The reason for this is that everyone—and I do mean everyone—walks around with some form of bias toward just about everything in life. That's right! Everyone has their own perception and opinion on things, and they're often not even aware that they're moving through life with this outlook. Your mom, for example, may see you as the most perfect person ever created, which is great, but it also means that she may not be able to see how debilitating your symptoms are for you.

How do we overcome other people's biases so that we can get proper feedback?

We set expectations and give clear instructions.

Here's an example: "I am working on my fear of being smelly and being mocked because of it. My goal is to shower twice a day for the next month and limit my time in the shower to 10 minutes. This compulsion causes me physical pain because I wash myself repeatedly until my skin hurts to make sure I am clean and smell great. I would like feedback on my behavior. This feedback should include how many times you notice me checking my body odor, how many times per day I shower, apply deodorant, or use other scents, and when you see me checking myself by smelling my clothing, skin, hair, or other parts of my body. I would like you to write this feedback down and not tell me in the moment, as I may become defensive and not respond well to the feedback."

As you can see from the example above, clear instructions have been given on the action you will take as well as what you expect from the people you've asked for help and feedback from. You've advised them of your goals, what behavior they can expect, and when not to give you feedback.

Now, there's a good reason for asking for feedback in this way, and that's because, just like everyone has their own perceptions and biases, everyone has the ability to take feedback negatively.

OCD teens, specifically, can react negatively to feedback for a couple of reasons, including

- a fear of rejection or failure.

- not trusting themselves to take feedback constructively.

- a fear that people won't like them as they change for the better.

- protecting their ego or not wanting to appear weak.

- a lack of emotional regulation, especially when faced with triggers.

So how do you learn to accept feedback and use it constructively in your journey toward mastering OCD? Take a look at the instructions below.

Instructions

1. Grab an A4 page and a pen or marker and write out the following phrase: "Receiving feedback and putting it to use takes time and practice!"

2. Put this page up where you can see it as a reminder that everyone needs some time to adjust to receiving feedback and applying it properly to their lives.

3. Fill in the table below until you're able to follow these steps without prompts or reacting to the feedback.

4. I have filled in the first column as an example for you.

Summarize	Ask	Respond	Commit	Reflect
Repeat the information you have received by summarizing what was said. *I did not achieve my goal of showering twice a day this week. This happened only once on a hot day when I was checking myself regularly.*	Check your understanding of this feedback by asking questions. *What do you think triggered my behavior? How could I interrupt the obsessions before the compulsion? How do you think I would've reacted?*	Respond thoughtfully. Don't react! Take a moment to digest the feedback. *On that day, I was experiencing a lot of stress. I felt uncomfortable in my own body because of the heat, but I didn't observe this when it happened.*	Commit to an action and communicate this action out loud by making a note. *On days when I feel a lot of stress, I will do my best to be more observant and aware. I will actively look for ways to manage this stress, like mindfulness.*	Once you have finished your feedback session, take time to reflect and adjust. *I have updated my milestones to reflect more stress management tools. I need to work on observing my*

				thoughts more often, as well as how my body feels.

Always remember that feedback should be constructive and not personal. If, after some time, you believe the person giving feedback is too personal or is focusing on personality, not behavior, you will need to take steps to stop the feedback.

Added to this, not *all* feedback needs to be used or instituted. Reflecting on the feedback received also means deciding whether or not this is something you need to work on right now, later, or not at all.

MBCT Exercise 3: Three-Minute Breathing Space

I've already spoken about mindfulness once in this book, and I'm sure you've heard about mindfulness practices, but perhaps you're confused about what they are exactly and why they're so beneficial.

A lot of the time, when we think about mindfulness, we imagine someone sitting on the ground, legs tangled in a knot, eyes closed, as they seemingly breathe into a state of bliss. Now, this is not entirely wrong, and if this is how you choose to become mindful, then more power to you. But mindfulness doesn't *require* you to meditate, be isolated, or contort yourself into any strange shape.

Mindfulness, or being mindful, is simply the ability to be aware and present in the moment without judgment or preconceived thoughts. It's the ability to pay attention to the sensations you're feeling as well as what you're thinking without reacting to them.

Being able to become mindful takes time, and there's a reason we call it "practicing mindfulness." This is why some people prefer to be alone and in silence so that they can free themselves of all distractions.

In fact, in the beginning stages of practicing mindfulness, it's best to find a quiet space so that you can fully benefit from the practice without too much stimulus around you. As you get better at the practice and can extend the time you spend in mindfulness, the more stimuli you can add to your environment.

Before we get into how to do this exercise, it's important that you know the different aspects of mindfulness. These are

- focusing on the present moment only.

- being non-judgmental of thoughts and sensations.

- being compassionate with yourself.

- accepting how you feel.

- being observant of patterns in thought and emotion.

- intentionally responding in a kind, rational way.

While mindfulness may sound like some hocus-pocus, mystical stuff, medicine, and psychology both endorse the practice as an incredibly powerful way to reduce stress and anxiety, over time and with practice, mindfulness helps us to build resilience, become clear about whether danger is real or not, and regulate our emotions.

The three-minute breathing exercise is designed to introduce you to the world of mindfulness practices. By setting aside three minutes, you can slowly introduce yourself to the world of observation and non-judgment. You can do this exercise multiple times a day, and as you begin to become better at the practice, you can extend your time in mindfulness as well or begin instituting different forms of mindfulness.

Instructions

1. Find a quiet space where you will be undisturbed for a full three minutes.

2. Sit down and make yourself comfortable. Don't slouch or lie down.

3. Set a timer for three minutes, and then place your phone face down, on silent, outside of your reach.

4. Close your eyes and take a deep breath—inhale through your nose and exhale through your mouth.

5. Bring your awareness to the present moment. Notice how your body feels, the thoughts you are having, and how you feel.

6. Don't try to change your thoughts, sensations, or feelings. Simply observe them for a count of 10.

7. Bring your focus to your breath. Take a deep breath, inhaling through your nose and then exhaling through your mouth. Notice how your body feels as oxygen fills your lungs. Feel the sensation of your belly rising and falling with every inhale and exhale.

8. Shift your awareness to your body. Begin at your toes and work your way slowly up your body until you reach the top of your head. Notice any sensations of tension you may be holding and breathe through these areas. Notice how your muscles relax with every cleansing breath.

9. Bring the focus back to your breath, repeating step 7, and fill your lungs with life-giving oxygen.

10. Shift your awareness to your thoughts and emotions. Notice how they pass through your mind, like clouds moving across the sky on a windy day. Don't try to focus on one thought or push it down; simply observe it and notice how it disappears before returning.

11. Return your focus to your breath, repeating step 7. Allow your body to fill with oxygen and feel the tension leave your body.

12. Now, bring your focus to awareness. Take a moment to scan your body. Notice how you feel and enjoy the sense of calm.

13. Take a deep breath and complete your exercise by affirming that you love yourself right now in this moment.

You can use your mindfulness exercise as many times a day as you need to help you remain calm, centered, and present.

MBCT Exercise 4: Mindful Eating

Remember when I mentioned that mindfulness can be practiced in just about any area of your life at almost any time? Mindful eating is an example of learning how to be mindful in any moment without having to remove ourselves from our environment to sit in isolation. While mindful eating may sound ridiculously easy to do, it can actually be quite challenging, especially when our OCD symptoms are triggered by food or eating rituals.

Before beginning our journey to mindful eating, it's important for us to know that the practice does so much more than aid digestion or slow us down to enjoy our food. In fact, mindful eating has the ability to become one of the most formidable tools available to us in our mindfulness journey as it brings more awareness to our body-mind connection.

For most teens, this body-mind connection can be compromised as we move through our teenage years at a frenetic pace and sometimes choose behaviors that we know aren't great for our bodies. For the OCD teen, this body-mind separation may be more severe than our counterparts as we look for ways to suppress not only our thoughts and emotions but the physically anxious sensations that accompany them.

When practicing mindful eating, we are reconnecting our mind and body, incorporating all of our senses to foster a much deeper awareness of how important it is to tap into our intuition and express self-love and gratitude.

Now, I know gratitude practices may sound like some fairytale exercise people do to live a life of denial about all the negative things that have happened to them, but neuroscience has actually proven that proper gratitude can actually rewire our brains for positive development.

When we live a life of proper gratitude, not in denial but in awe of all of the small things we can celebrate, reconnect our body and mind, and become non-judgmentally present, stress and anxiety reduce, helping us to cope with the thoughts that drive our compulsions.

The exercise below is designed to help you begin eating mindfully. To begin with, I suggest only practicing mindful eating once a day. The reason for this is that the practice is a lot harder than you think.

Remember to be patient with yourself as you learn to reconnect your body and mind, and keep in mind that we call this "practice" for a reason. It takes time and conscious effort to become a mindfulness pro, but the results are so worth it!

Instructions

1. Take a moment to calm your body before beginning your practice. Sit down and look at your food without judgment or preconceived thoughts.

2. Close your eyes and inhale deeply, holding your breath for a count of three before exhaling in a slow, controlled way through your mouth.

3. Open your eyes and observe your food. Don't label it by calling it names; just notice it, taking in the colors, textures, and shapes.

4. Close your eyes again and smell your food. Again, don't label the aromas; just enjoy the smells and allow them to fill your senses.

5. Draw attention to your body. How is it reacting to the food? Are you experiencing hunger sensations? Do you feel some excitement or curiosity?

6. Open your eyes and pick up your eating utensils. Feel the texture in your hand. Are they cool to the touch? How are your body and mind reacting to you touching your utensils? Do you feel any anticipation or excitement now?

7. Place a small, bite-sized piece of food on your utensil and engage all your senses again. What does it look, smell, sound, or even feel like on your utensil?

8. Bring the food to your mouth now. Notice how your senses engage when you place the food in your mouth. Chew slowly and deliberately, savoring the bite. Make sure to take note of the taste. Ask yourself, "What color does this taste like? What does it feel like in my mouth? How will this nourish my body?"

9. Before taking your next bite, stop for a moment and observe your body. How do you feel at this moment? Is your body or mind giving you cues about the food you're eating?

10. Now, take your next bite, repeating steps 6 through 9 until you are feeling satiated by your food.

11. When you are done eating, place your utensils on your plate. Notice the sound they make.

12. Observe your plate without judgment.

13. Say thanks for the food you have eaten by running through all of the positive sensations and feelings you experienced while eating.

14. Close your eyes once more. Take a deep breath in, holding it for a count of three before exhaling.

If a full meal is proving challenging, that's okay! Try to start small with a snack or even a drink before moving on to full meals.

MBCT Exercise 5: Sitting Meditation

Meditation, in all its forms, has been used for centuries as a way to become more mindful and improve physical and mental well-being. The other forms of mindfulness in this book have mostly focused on ways you can be mindful during your everyday life, but sitting meditation is different from these in two ways.

Firstly, this exercise will need to be completed as a dedicated practice in isolation rather than incorporating it wherever you are. The second reason it is different is that this exercise has almost nothing to do with OCD and everything to do with your mind and body.

Now, before you dismiss sitting meditation as a *useless* tool for you, hear me out.

Practicing sitting meditation is a great stress and anxiety buster; it helps to improve focus as well as concentration, increases self-awareness, and most importantly for you, facilitates emotional regulation.

Added to this, practicing sitting meditation improves resilience and boosts self-reflection skills, and all of this will help you become more aware of the sensations and stimuli that trigger obsessive thoughts. As an added bonus, sitting meditation increases feelings of relaxation, which affords you the opportunity to slow your anxious responses.

Okay, so now you know that sitting meditation is a *deliberate* practice, and like everything else in life that requires practice, you need time and consistency to become really great at it. Because of this, I suggest setting aside 10 minutes every day, either first thing in the morning or last thing at night, to practice sitting meditation.

Instructions

1. Find a quiet, comfortable, and dedicated space for your sitting meditation. A lot of people have created a meditation space in their bedroom where they feel safe, calm, and relaxed. Feel free to do the same. Alternatively, sit comfortably on the floor or a chair.

2. Set a timer for 5 minutes. You will work your way up to 10 minutes in increments.

3. Once seated, correct your posture. Your spine should be straight, and your shoulders should be back. Make sure you are comfortable but not slouched over.

4. Place your hand's palm down on your thighs.

5. Take a deep, cleansing breath, inhaling through your nose.

6. Hold this breath for a count of four and exhale through your mouth.

7. Bring your gaze down to your hands so that you don't become distracted by anything in your environment.

8. Draw your focus to your breath, noticing the sensation as your lungs fill with oxygen.

9. Begin to notice how your body responds to your breathing. Focus on the rise and fall of your belly.

10. When thoughts enter your mind, acknowledge them but do not engage them. Simply notice that they're there and allow them to float through your mind.

11. If your thoughts begin to distract you, draw your focus back to your breath. Deliberately inhale deeply, holding your breath for a count of three. And exhaling slowly.

12. Once you feel calm, begin to expand your awareness. Draw your focus on your hands and your fingers first, slowly moving your gaze upward.

13. Hold your focus on something in your room for a count of 20.

14. Notice the shapes, colors, and textures that make up this object. Don't label it; simply notice that it exists.

15. Now, bring your focus back to your breath.

16. Take a deep breath in, inhaling through your nose, for a count of five.

17. Hold this breath for a count of three.

18. Exhale slowly, allowing all of the oxygen to leave your body.

19. Focus on breathing normally.

20. Take a moment to adjust to your surroundings and continue with your day.

If you're having trouble sitting for a full 5 minutes, gradually build up to 5 minutes and, finally, to ten minutes.

MBCT Exercise 6: Body Scanning

We already covered progressive muscle relaxation (PMR) in Chapter 1. Body scanning is an expansion of this technique to help increase your awareness and control over your body's sensations.

Practicing body scanning comes with a whole lot of benefits for managing the symptoms of OCD and sets us up for becoming adults who already have the right tools and techniques to cope with the stresses and strains of being a grown-up.

So what does body scanning do for you, and how does it differ from the PMR exercise you've already learned?

Up to this point, you have learned how to deepen your conscious thought awareness. Body scanning creates a deeper awareness of your body by bringing attention not only to the sensations you're feeling but also by showing you that you *do* have control over your body.

By understanding your mind-body connection more deeply, you can begin to strengthen this connection and learn to calm your anxiety and manage your stress better. Once you become a pro at body scanning, you will actually develop the ability to actively promote relaxation not just in your body but in your mind too.

This active relaxation ability is achieved through mindfulness and being able to tap into each muscle in your body, releasing pent-up energy as well as muscle tension. This is especially useful for teens who may experience pain from their bodies tensing as a result of anxiety and stress.

Body scanning is the ultimate level of body-mind integration, encouraging your mind to positively influence your body into facilitating positive behaviors. A healthy mind and body foster a positive relationship with yourself, and you will begin to want to take care of yourself and honor your body and mind so that you truly encompass what it means to have well-being.

Before you begin your body scanning exercise, remember that it is a practice. Try to remain neutral and do not judge your body while practicing. If your inner critic begins saying negative things about the area of your body you're focusing on, challenge it by saying out loud, "I love this body I am in."

It's best to do your body scanning exercise at the very end of the day when it doesn't matter if you fall asleep or not. If you do fall asleep, that's fine—in fact, most people never complete a full body scan because it's so relaxing!

Instructions

1. Lie down on your bed.

2. Get into a comfortable position on your back.

3. Make sure your body is properly supported and that you have blankets on your body in case you fall asleep.

4. Close your eyes and focus on your breath.

5. Inhale through your nose and exhale through your mouth.

6. Now, inhale deeply for a count of five, holding your breath for a count of three.

7. Exhale deeply for a count of six.

8. Repeat your deep breathing five times.

9. Direct your attention to your toes. Squeeze your toes and only your toes, holding this squeezed position for a count of 10.

10. Notice the sensation as you release the tension in your toes.

11. Take a deep breath and exhale.

12. Draw attention to your feet. Point or flex your feet and hold this position for a count of 10.

13. Notice the sensation in your feet as you release the position.

14. Move up to your calves and repeat, tensing for a count of ten before releasing and noticing the sensation.

15. Do this with every area of your body—toes, feet, calves, thighs, glutes, belly, shoulders, arms, hands, fingers, jaw, and face.

16. Remember to breathe after every tense and released muscle so that you give your mind a chance to reset and focus on the next area of your body.

17. A lot of the time, people fall asleep before they even reach their arms, and if this is the case for you, it's perfectly normal.

18. It doesn't matter when you wake up from your body-scanning exercises. What is important is to notice how relaxed your body feels.

19. If you do manage to get through your entire body, end your practice by drawing focus back to your breath once more, inhaling deeply, and exhaling in a controlled manner.

Regular practice of body scanning will help you to truly enhance your awareness of the stimuli and triggers that cause you anxiety and may heighten your OCD symptoms. And if you aren't quite at the body scanning level yet, that's absolutely fine. Using any mindfulness technique will only help you become more aware and develop a deeper understanding of just how capable you are of managing your OCD symptoms.

Conclusion

OCD can feel like a life sentence we have received for something we didn't do. It's challenging, overwhelming, and at times, can feel devastating to have to deal with. Our minds and bodies seem resistant to playing along, and on some level, we do know that our compulsions are not helping us, but still, we give into them in the hopes that they will calm the storm in our minds.

Our friends and family can find it difficult to empathize with what we are going through and how dramatically our lives can be disrupted by the symptoms of OCD. We experience academic challenges as we find it difficult to concentrate, and the pressure to succeed overwhelms us.

We worry about what others will think of us, and our compulsions interfere with our friendships and other relationships, destroying our self-confidence and our ability to be fully independent, even though we crave social isolation.

Of course, this all leads to extreme emotional distress that compounds over time as our awareness becomes more and more focused on our thoughts. Our self-esteem all but leaves, and we live in a perpetual state of anxiety, emotional instability, and lowered self-esteem.

While medical intervention and professional treatment are absolutely necessary to help us improve our symptoms and well-being, it is also important that we play an active role in our own lives.

There are so many steps we can take to manage our symptoms, and I applaud every one of you who has read this book and started completing the exercises in it. Education is key, but action has the ability to open the door to a much brighter future in which our OCD no longer controls us.

With the help of different forms of therapy as well as bringing awareness to our thoughts in an empathetic, non-judgmental way, we can begin to live a life in which we thrive rather than treading water to survive.

Before you turn to the last page of this book and begin to focus on the exercises and worksheets that will help you improve your well-being, there's something really important you should know.

You are so much more resilient, brave, and strong than you think. OCD isn't a challenge you should have to face, and I know it can feel like an insurmountable obstacle at times, but you have an inner strength that many others do not.

You have already overcome so much, and I am so proud of you for acknowledging your responsibility in managing your symptoms. It takes an enormous amount of courage to stare OCD in the eye and let it know that you are stronger than anything it may throw your way.

Reading this book and practicing these exercises is a significant step toward understanding your OCD better, and with understanding comes knowledge of how to overcome it.

There will be times when you feel like giving up… when the intrusive thoughts are the loudest voice in the room of your mind, and that is fine. The journey to any destination is very rarely linear, nor is it without the occasional detour.

Here's the thing about life: It's fraught with challenges, but it also has so much beauty and joy in it. You're going to experience ups and downs; that's just the way it is, but every conscious, brave, and resilient step you take toward your managed OCD journey is one that is going to bring you closer to your goal.

Remember, it's the small actions we take and the positive choices we make that improve our lives, and while it may feel like things are taking forever, it's important to understand that life is a journey with no specific destination.

Instead, it's a winding road that we take to several destinations that we call goals. Each mile we travel is a milestone we can cross off on this journey, and every setback should be seen as an opportunity to learn but also to stop for a moment so that we can see how far we have come.

You are not alone on this journey called life either, and just because others don't necessarily understand exactly what we're going through, they will be there to support us if we openly communicate how we feel and ask for their feedback.

This brings me to my next point. Surround yourself with people who love you, inspire you, and will lift you up when you stumble or fall because they are the people who can see your potential. They'll encourage you to tap into your inner courage and show you just how capable you are of overcoming just about anything in life.

Love yourself fiercely no matter how low you feel because nothing silences an inner critic better than the awe-inspiring power of self-love and acceptance. Remind yourself daily of how unique you are—of the talents you have, how strong you are, and how unique your particular life is.

And I know it's super clichéd, but the darkest moments in our lives have the potential to show us how incredibly bright our inner light is. You are capable, you are powerful, and you have the ability to achieve greatness in absolutely anything you set your mind to, and I promise you, the challenges you are facing now will forge you into a superhero.

You've got this, teen! You will overcome OCD, and while the condition is lifelong, it is *not* a life sentence. You have done nothing wrong, and OCD was never your fault. There is a way through this maze you're experiencing, and you will overcome it so that you can thrive and become the best version of yourself that you can possibly be.

It is absolutely within the realm of possibility for you to live a happy, joyful life. Will there be challenges? Of course, but with support, treatment, and a whole lot of self-care, there is no reason you cannot manage your symptoms and live a wonderful life.

Now go ahead and shine like the supernova star you are—free your mind, empower your true self, and unleash your full potential!

References

ABC Funtional Analysis. (n.d.-a). Positive Psychology. chrome-extension://efaidnbmnnnibpcajpcglclefindmkaj/https://positive.b-cdn.net/wp-content/uploads/2020/09/ABC-Functional-Analysis-Worksheet.pdf

Decatastrophizing. (n.d.-b). Positive Psychology. https://www.therapistaid.com/worksheets/decatastrophizing

Effective Feedback Workshop. (2023). Session Lab. https://www.sessionlab.com/blog/effective-feedback-workshop/

Index-The Complete Set of Client Handouts and Worksheets from ACT books by Russ Harris ACT Made Simple 3 The Confidence Gap 21 The Happiness Trap 26. (n.d.). Act Mindfully. https://www.actmindfully.com.au/upimages/2016_Complete_Worksheets_for_Russ_Harris_ACT_Books.pdf

Obsessive Compulsive Disorder (OCD) Worksheets. (2015). Psychology Tools. https://www.psychologytools.com/professional/problems/obsessive-compulsive-disorder-ocd/

Segal, Z. (2016, June 8). *The Three-Minute Breathing Space Practice.* Mindful. https://www.mindful.org/the-three-minute-breathing-space-practice/

Thought Defusion cognitive distancing techniques. (n.d.). Therapist Aid. https://www.therapistaid.com/worksheets/thought-defusion-techniques

Zauderer, S. (2023, January 11). *57+ OCD Statistics: How Many People Have OCD?* Cross River Therapy. https://www.crossrivertherapy.com/ocd-statistics#:~:text=People%20Have%20OCD%3F-

Made in the USA
Las Vegas, NV
17 October 2023

79223416R00052